More titles in this series:

Archaeologists and What They Do
Astronauts and What They Do
Astronomers and What They Do
Bakers and What They Do
Ballerinas and What They Do
Beekeepers and What They Do
Chefs and What They Do
Construction Workers and What They Do
Dentists and What They Do
Doctors and What They Do

Firefighters and What They Do
Nurses and What They Do
Optometrists and What They Do
Park Rangers and What They Do
Pilots and What They Do
Race Car Drivers and What They Do
Teachers and What They Do
Truck Drivers and What They Do
Veterinarians and What They Do

With special thanks to Nele and Peter, cargo ship officers.
For Leon, who loves crane vessels.
For Liene, who likes traveling on cruise ships.

Copyright © 2023 Clavis Publishing Inc., New York

Originally published as *De kapitein* in Belgium and the Netherlands by Clavis Uitgeverij, 2022
English translation from the Dutch by Clavis Publishing Inc., New York

Visit us on the Web at www.clavis-publishing.com.

Ship Captains and What They Do written by and illustrated by Liesbet Slegers

ISBN 978-1-60537-963-0

This book was printed in August 2023 at Nikara, M. R. Štefánika 858/25, 963 01 Krupina, Slovakia.

First Edition
10 9 8 7 6 5 4 3 2 1

Clavis Publishing supports the First Amendment and celebrates the right to read.

Ship Captains
and What They Do

Liesbet Slegers

Clavis

NEW YORK

A ship can transport all kinds of things.

An airplane pilot flies people or stuff through the air. A truck driver transports things on highways. But most transportation is done by ship, over water. There are different kinds of ships. Some carry passengers, cars, sand, wood, or grain. Others transport containers filled with all kinds of things. Besides passenger ships and cargo ships, there are cruise ships, sailboats, fishing vessels, and many more. It's the **ship captain**, also called the **skipper**, and the crew who steer a boat. Will you join us to see what they do?

The skipper of an inland vessel does all kinds of chores outside on the deck of the boat. This is done safely with work clothes and also shoes with a steel tip.

At sea, there are often very large ships that transport people or things all over the world. We call this **maritime transport**. Many people work on a seagoing vessel. Everyone has their own task on the ship. The captain is the boss. There are also boats that sail into a country on canals and rivers. That's called **inland transport**. On those boats, the captain, or skipper, wears a uniform and a captain's hat. The skipper often wears comfortable clothes to steer the boat, or work clothes and work shoes. Together with the sailors, the skipper does all kinds of chores. Of course, there are also life vests on board for safety.

the ship captain's hat

the life vest

comfortable clothes
and shoes

the captain's uniform: pants and jacket
with four gold stripes (one of which
has a curl), indicating the captain's rank

the mooring lines

the wharf

the bollard

If you get off the boat over the gangway, you arrive on the wharf. That's the place right beside the water, usually made out of stone or wood. The boat is tied to the wharf with mooring lines.

The captain needs a lot to get the job done. First of all, a boat, of course! From the wheelhouse, the skipper has a good view of the boat and the water. In the **wheelhouse** are a **compass** and **GPS** as well as more gadgets to help the crew steer and sail properly. There are **lifebuoys** and **lifeboats** in case someone falls overboard, but luckily that doesn't happen very often. With the **mooring lines** (cables and ropes), the crew ties the ship to the **bollards** on the wharf. The **anchor** is used to stop the ship at sea. The **radar** picks up signals from other ships and also indicates where lighthouses and even icebergs are. This way, the captain knows exactly what's around, so the ship doesn't bump into something. How clever!

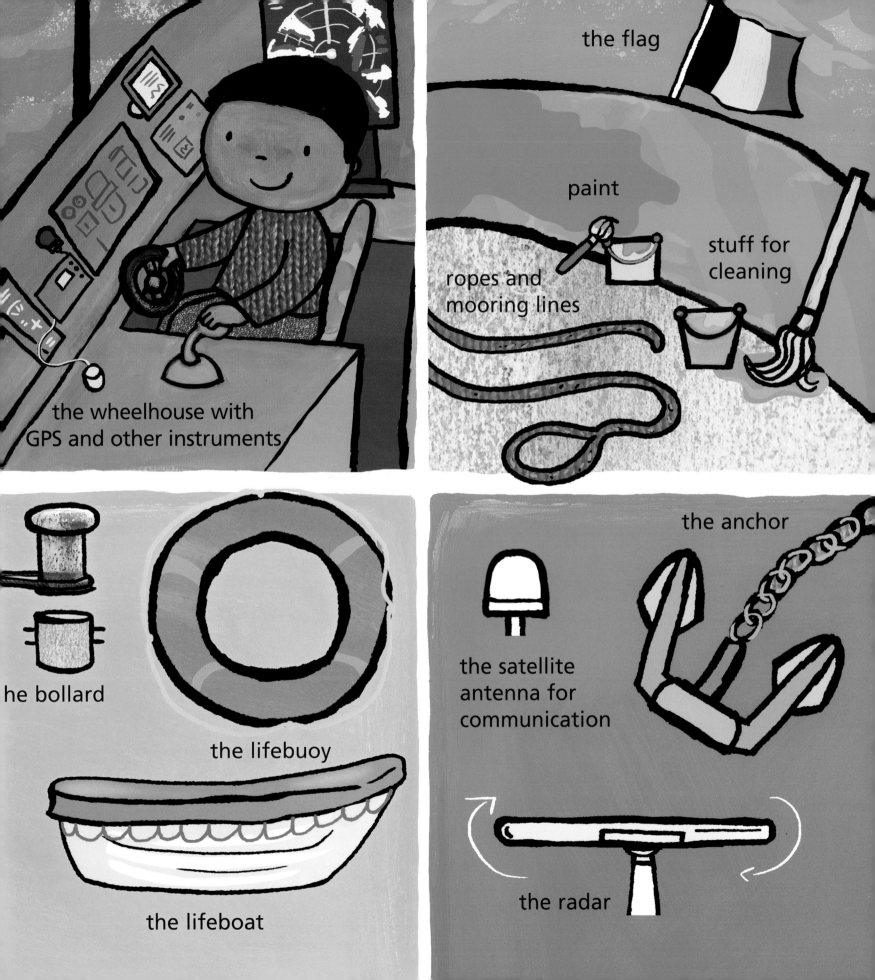

the wheelhouse with GPS and other instruments

the flag

paint

ropes and mooring lines

stuff for cleaning

he bollard

the lifebuoy

the lifeboat

the anchor

the satellite antenna for communication

the radar

At sea, the captain is in charge of the many crew members.

the engineer

the cook

the sailor

The ship's captain is sailing at sea with a large container ship. In the many containers, there are goods that are transported from faraway countries. This is called **cargo**. On board, everyone has their own task: The cook provides the food, and the engineer takes care of the engine and the machines in the belly of the ship. The sailor stands guard, cleans, and does all kinds of chores. The captain and the officers steer the ship from the wheelhouse. They look over the containers and keep a close eye on the instruments in the wheelhouse. The containers take up most of the space on the ship, but there's also a place for everyone to sleep, eat, and bathe. There's even a small pharmacy, in case someone gets sick or injured at sea.

*The **engines** ensure that the propeller is turning. Fuel is needed to make the engines work.*

*The **propeller** turns and moves the boat forward or backward. To **brake**, the propeller turns **in the opposite direction**.*

*The **rudder**, underwater at the back, steers the boat.*

After sailing for a long time, the ocean vessel arrives at the harbor where the containers will be unloaded. It's difficult for a large ship to dock in a port, so someone arrives by helicopter or a small boat and helps steer the ship. This is the **ship pilot**. The ship pilot knows all the shallow and dangerous places and helps bring the ship safely into port. **Tugboats** often also help. They push or pull the large ship in the right direction.

With strong, heavy rope or cables called mooring lines, the crew members tie the ship to the wharf.

When the ship arrives at the wharf, the **crew members** tie the mooring lines to the bollards. This makes sure the ship stays in the right place and keeps it from drifting away. The captain signals that all the containers can be taken off the ship. A big crane puts them all on the wharf. Smaller inland vessels or trucks will transport the containers to their next destination via rivers and canals. After the container ship is loaded up again, it's ready to start the next job and return to sea. Good work, captain and all your crew!

The skipper loads the car off the inland vessel onto the wharf. With the car, the skipper or sailor can go shopping.

Of course, a seagoing vessel is much too big to sail inland, which means into the country. Therefore, inland vessels each collect a part of the cargo from the seagoing vessel for the next leg of the journey. Inland vessels are much smaller and can easily sail on rivers and canals. On this cozy boat, these sailors live with their two children and their dog. In the little house, they can sleep, cook, and take a shower. Even their car sails along! "Come on, kids," says the skipper. "I'll take you to the skipper school." The children stay at a special overnight school for kids of sailors who will be away for a couple of days.

The big cranes in the harbor are so cool!

The inland vessel is refueled so that the engines can run. The skipper departs to pick up a load of containers at the port. The large crane in the port neatly stacks the containers one by one onto the inland vessel. Once it's loaded, the vessel sails from the harbor to an inland factory or other final destination for its cargo.

On board an inland vessel, there's often a sailor as well. The sailor helps the skipper and sometimes has his own cabin at the front of the ship.

The sailing route has been set, and the mooring lines have been untied. Now the fully loaded inland vessel can depart. While the ship is sailing, the wheelhouse is up high. This allows the skipper to look over the stacked containers and see where the ship is going. The sailor cleans the deck, which has become dirty from loading. (After loading loose sand, for example, there can be a lot of cleanup to do!) Washed clothes can now dry outside in the wind. The skipper's dog barks at a seagull.

Some bridges, called drawbridges, open for the inland vessel.

If a bridge is high enough, the boat can sail under it.

The skipper keeps a close eye on the computer screens in the wheelhouse. The small steering wheel is used to control the ship. Calls can also be made to other skippers sailing nearby. If a bridge is high enough, the skipper can sail under it. Meanwhile, the cars on top of the bridge just keep on driving. But some bridges are too low. These are opened, so that the ship can pass through. The cars then have to wait until the bridge can be lowered again. It's a good thing there are drawbridges!

Starboard and **port** indicate the sides of a ship. If you stand on a ship and face forward, the left side is called the port, and the right side is the starboard.

After sailing for a long time, the skipper needs a rest. He goes to sleep in a warm bed on the ship.

At night, the lights on a boat shine clearly. This is important for everyone's safety. There's a green light on the starboard side and a red light on the port side. At the top of the mast or the wheelhouse, and also at the back, a white light shines. That way, someone on another boat knows exactly which side of the ship is shining in the dark. How clever!

Soon the containers will be unloaded. And tomorrow the children can be picked up from the skipper school. What fun it is to work and live on a ship. Thank you, skipper, for your work on the water!

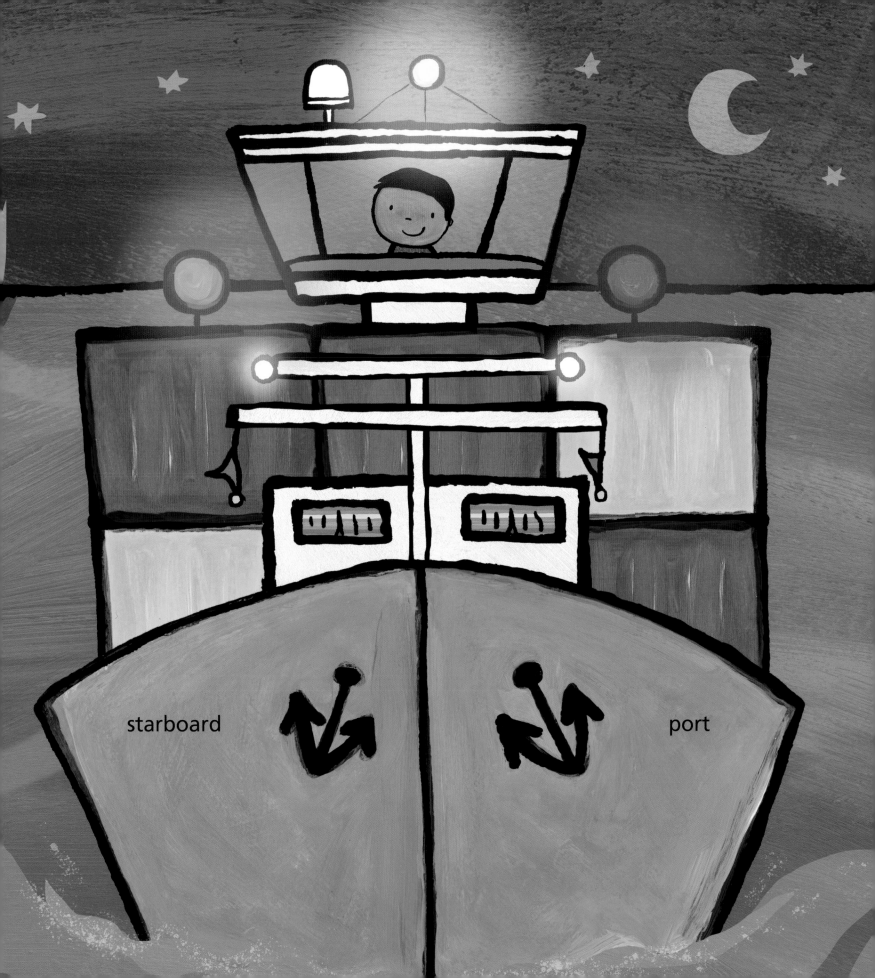

What's a lock?

The water isn't always the same level in rivers and canals. In one river, the water can be high, and in another river, the water can be low. When a boat has to go from a low river to a high one (or vice versa), it needs some kind of elevator. That's the lock! It helps the boat go up or down. The lock has traffic lights, just like roads do. The lock is operated by the **lockkeeper**. She sits high up in a house on the wharf. That way, she can see everything clearly and operate the lock. Would you like to see how a lock works?

The boat is almost at the lock.
The skipper and the lockkeeper are talking on the phone.

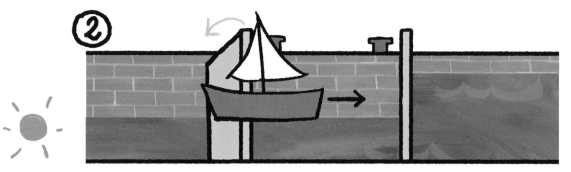

When the water in the middle section is as high as the boat, the first **lock gate** opens. The light changes to green. The boat moves into the middle section, called the **lock chamber**. Then the first lock gate closes again.

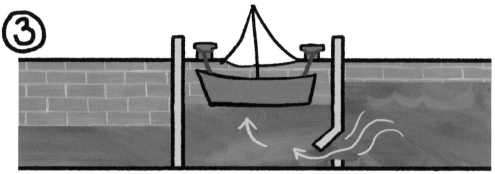

The boat is tied to bollards with mooring lines. This keeps the boat safely in place. Then a hatch at the bottom of the second lock gate opens. This allows water to flow in. The water under the boat rises—and the boat rises with it!

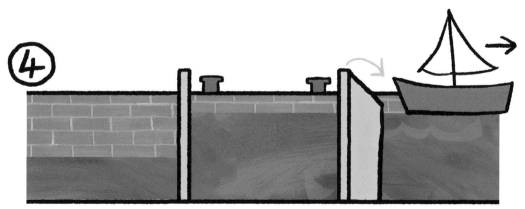

Now the water the boat sits on is as high as the water where the boat wants to go. The mooring lines are untied again. The second lock gate opens. The boat can move on. Have a good trip!

Ahoy! What belongs together?

At the top of this page are the wind, a suitcase, and a fish. At the bottom are three kinds of ships. What belongs to which boat? Do you know why?

A sailboat with sails catches the wind, which makes the boat move forward.

A fishing boat has large nets to catch fish with.

On a cruise ship, many people can go on vacation at the same time. On board, it's fun, and along the way, there are a lot of beautiful things to see!